IT ALL STARTS WITH A BUDGET!

The building blocks to build a better financial future!

DEDICATION

I dedicate this book to my Women's Ministry Financial Spring 2018 Class! The thought for this book truly grew out of this class! Thank you Franklin Avenue Baptist Church for allowing me to use my gifts and talents!

And major thanks to my family – you continue to support me in everything I do no matter what – that means everything to me!

Table of Contents

Introduction

Start today!

Many years ago, when I found myself in thousands of dollars in credit card debt, I simply didn't know what to do. I thought to myself there is no way in the world I'll ever be able to get out of this debt and simply thought it would always be this way.

But one day, I felt God tugging at my heart. He led me to a scripture that I often refer to when I have trouble with choosing faith instead of fear - it is Luke 1:37 (KJV), "For with God nothing shall be impossible. This scripture became my foundation and my Word in due season. It gave me a sense of power that with God anything is possible. So for that reason - I stood on His Word.

I made a commitment to make the necessary steps to eliminate my debt. I knew the road would not be easy but at that moment I knew it was possible. So I set out on one of the most challenging journeys in my life, but in the end, I was victorious.

I first started with praying to God and asking Him for His help during this time. I then began to write out all of my debts on paper. I arranged the debts from the highest interest rates to the lowest. Finally, I divided the debt by twelve (12) to get an idea of the amount I needed to pay each month and subsequently pay off the entire balance by year-end.

That moment I could have fallen to the floor (lol). I thought, "How would I be able to do this?" But then it dawned on me - I had to start with a budget. So I did.

For the next twelve (12) months, I created a budget each month and tracked my spending like no other. I knew that I couldn't afford to misappropriate a single dollar if I was to reach my goal. Also, I found additional ways to earn income (I will discuss this in a later chapter). At that moment, I knew if I wanted to reach my goals – I had to not only create a budget but stick to it. Why? Because the misappropriation of one single dollar would cause me to overspend and not have enough money to meet my monthly target payoff goal.

I must admit that year was a great challenge for me. Towards the end of the year, I gave up once or twice but quickly got back on track. At the end of the year, I paid off my credit cards and finally was credit card debt free!

There is no way around it. If you want to reach your financial goals – you have to start with a budget. It is only then will you be able to get out of debt, save more money, put aside money for retirement or even start your dream business! Remember it all starts with a budget!

Prelude

During the past few years, I have had the honor to teach in my church women's ministry classes, led by our pastor's wife. She has a special calling to help members find and use their spiritual gifts, which has allowed me to share my gift with the Body of Christ.

The last time I was asked to teach, I had to make a big decision, whether to teach or not. The class was scheduled the same day of the week I was to teach an accounting course at a university where I worked. After praying and seeking God, I knew God was leading me to teach at my church – so I did. Unknowingly to many, I asked the university to find a replacement and volunteered my time with the women's class. And as I write this prelude, I couldn't be more thankful! Had I not taught that class this book would not have come to pass!

While teaching that financial biblical study, I realized there was one saying that I kept repeating throughout the class and also to my clients – "It all starts with a budget!"

During that time, I sought God concerning the next steps for my life. I knew He was telling me to write this book. But more importantly, shortly after He gave me the title, as I was reading another biblical resource, I fell upon these words - It all starts with God! I was literally like – Whoa!

I knew in that moment, He was providing me with confirmation about the next steps I should take. I share this story with you because it is so important that you seek God first in all things (Matthew 6:33)! Not only seek Him, but have a relationship with His Son, Jesus Christ.

Please understand, it wasn't until I surrendered my plans and asked Him, "What would you have me to do?," that I started writing for major media publications, appearing on the news, authoring my books and starting my business! The list can go on! I am grateful that I surrendered to Him because He knows just what is best for me!

While I know this book is about budgeting, I would be a disservice if I didn't share this story. It wasn't until I truly surrendered my life to Him that God opened doors that I would never in a million years (not even with my talent or education) be able to open! I do believe God has a way of ordering our steps even when we are not expecting it. It is only when I began to give my life to Him that everything else fell into place.

If you want to live your best, know which direction to go and live out your purpose here on Earth - give your life to Christ! Simply acknowledge Him as Lord and Savior, believe He died for your sins, and confess your sins before Him (Romans 10:9)! I promise, it will be the best decision you will ever make!

How to use this book

Throughout this book, I share how to use my financial planner, "Are you wearing the B.A.D.G.E. ®?" This planner is a great supplement to this book as you get your finances in order. In addition, the planner provides monthly worksheets for budgeting, money tracking, a bill calendar, debt pay down sheets and more. This book refers to the planner to help you reach your goals.

Also, if you have ever taken one of my classes, you know that I believe in having an accountability partner with you throughout your journey! Find someone who can come along for the ride as we explore the building blocks to not only a better budget but a better financial life.

Your partner:

_____

@Kemwashcpa

#kemcents

The B.A.D.G.E. ®

My personal finance blog, Kemberley.com is based on five (5) key principles I believe are necessary to obtain a financial healing. These five (5) principles have not only been a blessing to others, but have also been a blessing to myself to get my own personal finances in order. I refer to these principles as the B-A-D-G-E ®!

This book is the first of a five-part series to help you with these principles. In addition, I refer often to the B.A.D.G.E. ® financial planner throughout the book and suggest you use it along with this book to help you keep your finances in order, create your budget for each period, track your expenses, monitor your financial progress and more.

A badge is defined as a means of identification and it informs others how you identify yourself. As you travel on your financial journey and make difficult financial decisions, you must wear the B-A-D-G-E ®!

B – Budget:
It all starts with a budget

In order to get the most out of your finances, you have to create and stick to a budget. And not just every now and then. You must budget consistently. Budgeting provides an understanding of the purpose of every dollar that comes into your possession! Not only does a budget gives you an understanding of how to use your money, but it also provides a blueprint of what you can or cannot afford.

For which of you, intending to build a tower, does not sit down first and count the cost, whether he has enough to finish it—lest, after he has laid the foundation, and is not able to finish, all who see it begin to mock him, saying, 'This man began to build and was not able to finish'?

(Luke 14:28-30 NKJ)

A-Assets:
You make a lot, but how much do you keep?

Everyone has the ability to earn money, but increasing your wealth is true financial freedom. Wealth, which is defined as your assets minus your liabilities. Thus the more assets and the fewer liabilities - the better! Building wealth is the gateway to opportunities. Wealth allows for creating entrepreneurship, funding your children's education, purchasing a home and leaving an inheritance for your children's children!

A good man leaves an inheritance to his children's children. But the wealth of the sinner is stored up for the righteous.

(Proverbs 13:22 NKJV)

D – Debt:
Be the lender and not the borrower

Debt is the enemy of any financial healing. Having too much debt or using debt unwisely can cost more than you bargained for. Of course, there is some debt you may have to obtain in life, however, there are other forms of debt you should simply stay away from. Using debt can either enhance your financial life or destroy it. Be mindful of every loan, credit card, or mortgage you obtain. Determine whether the debt will move you closer to your financial goals or further away.

The Lord will open to you His good treasure, the heavens, to give the rain to your land in its season, and to bless all the work of your hand. You shall lend to many nations, but you shall not borrow.

(Deuteronomy 28:12 NKJV)

G – Goals:
Write the vision and it shall run

If you don't know where you are going you won't
know how to get there. Many people do not use a
holistic approach when it comes to finances. As a
result, they have investments or assets that do not
align with their goals. Know both your short-term
and long-term goals and identify how you will get
there. Simply put, create a plan for your money
and even more important – for your life!

The plans of the diligent lead surely to plenty,
But those of everyone who is hasty, surely to
poverty.

(Proverbs 21:5 NKJV)

**"If you don't know where you are going, you won't
know how to get there."**

@Kemwashcpa

#kemcents

E – Earnings:
What's in your possession?

While wealth builds opportunities, enhancing your earning potential is also key to success. Earnings provide a gateway to be able to build a better financial life. Creating multiple streams of income and increasing your potential to earn more will allow you to obtain a financial breakthrough. Lastly, make certain to partner with God with your earnings. Commit to tithing and stand on His promises, knowing He will open the windows of heaven for you!

Bring all the tithes into the storehouse, that there may be food in My house, And try Me now in this," Says the Lord of hosts, "If I will not open for you the windows of heaven. And pour out for you such blessing that there will not be room enough to receive it."

(Malachi 3:10 NKJV)

So, now that you have an understanding of the entire B.A.D.G.E. ®, let's us dive into the first part of the B.A.D.G.E.®, and explore what the "B" (budget principle) of the B-A-D-G-E®, is all about!

Shall we?

START WITH HIM!

Matthew 6:33

CHAPTER 1

Building Block #1:

Start with Him!

But seek ye first the kingdom and his righteousness, and all these things shall be added unto you.

(Matthew 6:33 KJV)

I can recall in my late teens attending a prayer meeting with my mother. At that time, an older lady called me out and said, "Seek ye first the kingdom of God and all things shall be added to you." I nodded at the time in agreement, but honestly, I had no idea what that really meant.

Seek Him First

However, I remember learning this lesson early on in life. God allowed me to purchase my first home at the age of 23, and this experience taught me so much. During that time, I fell in love with a home I really wanted. I was so excited about purchasing this home, but shortly after praying, the opportunity fell through. I was devastated.

Later, I was able to find a home that was great and I knew the moment I found it – it was the home for me. As years went by, I realized why God closed that door. The neighborhood for the first home became infested with crime and the values of those homes quickly declined. That taught me a lesson early on – seek God first – not just for some things – but in all things! But how do we really do this concerning our money?

Financial Healing Prayer

First, start with prayer. Understanding my need for God to intervene in my personal finances many years ago- I began to locate scriptures in the Bible as it relates to my financial situation. This is something I still practice today. I often find scriptures that relate to whatever I am going through and simply give God back His Word!

In doing so - I continue to find victory through Him and know that all things work together for my good! Remember, His Word reminds us that it is powerful and sharper than any two edge sword!

So what's your prayer? What scriptures can you stand on as it relates to your finances? When it comes to your finances, find scriptures that relate specifically to your goals you are attempting to achieve during this time in your life. Whether it is to become a better steward, tither, or budget more - create a personal prayer or declaration to God you can recite daily. Here is my prayer...

Financial Healing Prayer

Heavenly Father, we come to You worshipping You in spirit and in truth (John 4:23-24). We ask today for forgiveness for our financial mistakes. We thank You for giving us another chance to be financial stewards. You say in Your Word, if we are faithful over little, we will be trusted with much (Luke 16:10).

We declare this day going forward, we will operate with a financial plan (Luke 14:28-30). We declare that we will set aside a portion of every dime that comes into our possession, so that we may prosper (1 Corinthians 16:2).

We promise to be diligent in both our financial and business affairs (Proverb 10:4). We thank You for all of our financial blessings and declare that we are content with what You have already blessed us with (Hebrews 13:5).

We declare from this day forward to be the lender and not the borrower (Deuteronomy 15:6) and that our debts are cancelled and dissolved. We promise to tithe and give to those in need (Proverbs 21:26), knowing we will receive (Malachi 3:10). We cease from worrying because we know you will supply all our needs according to your riches (Philippians 4:19). God, we know in all things we will prosper even in the land of drought (Jeremiah 17:8). In Jesus Christ of Nazareth's name, we pray.

Amen (John 14:14).

@kemwashcpa #kemcents

Tithing God's Way

Next, I knew if I wanted to put God first in my finances, I had to commit to tithing. In His Word, He tells us that we are to bring ten (10) percent of our money to the kingdom of God! While that may seem like a lot, in reality, it is not much at all. If God gives us the ability to earn, what is giving Him back just a dime of a dollar that He has already so graciously provided?

I can recall in my years right after college, I decided I wanted to tithe. I grew up in a household where I witnessed my mother tithed no matter what! So when I obtained my first full-time job after college I too began to tithed.

However, when my change was a "little strange," I decided not to tithe for the period and tell God, "Okay, I'll catch you next month!" To be honest, the fact of the matter was - it wasn't that I couldn't afford to tithe, I was simply being wasteful with my money. I was operating without a budget and as such, I would spend my money here and there. I was a victim to impulsive shopping and spending.

And even worse, every time my favorite store had a one-day sale (which it had every other day), I would be committed to obtaining things I really didn't need!

After realizing this ~ I knew it was time to make a change! It was during these times my change was strange and things truly fell out of place. So from that moment, I committed to tithe no matter what!!

Now let me warn you ~ I don't tithe just to obtain great financial blessings from God. I tithe out of obedience. This is important to understand because there will be some times when you may wonder if you should stay committed or not! I have experienced moments where I was truly faithful despite financial challenges and I chose to be obedient.

Not long after, I would receive a blessing that I was not expecting to received. Not only this, I do believe when we choose to be obedient, it is not only in finances that He blesses us! He gives us peace, health, love, salvation, joy and so much more! So, I must also tell you ~ there are blessings when we do tithe!!! He promises in His Word that He will pour out a blessing that we simply do not have room enough to receive (Malachi 3:10)!!

Reflection

Write out a declaration concerning your finances using scriptures as it relates to financial obstacles you desire to overcome. Declare and read it daily.

START WITH A VISION!

Habakkuk 2:2

CHAPTER 2

Building Block #2:

→

Start with a vision!

And the Lord answered me, and said, Write the vision, and make it plain upon tables, that he may run that readeth it.

(Habakkuk 2:2 KJV)

This is one of my favorite verses. It reminds us that if we write the vision down and make it plain — it will run! This holds true for our finances as well. We have to write out our budgets so that we can have a plan of action for our money before we spend a dollar from our pay.

Not only write out our budgets but track our expenses (we will discuss more of this in Chapter 4). But let me just ask you a question. If I asked you, how much did you spend this month on eating out, would you be able to tell me? If I asked what amount did you pay on your total bills last month, do you know?

Chances are, if you don't keep a budget or monitor your expenses, you are simply threading the unknown. However, if you do keep a record of your spending, you have an idea of what you shelled out last month!

Not every dollar is made for spending

During my college years, I simply thought every dollar that came into my possession was made for spending. To make matters worse, I owned all of the latest designer fashions. Well, shall I say borrowed, because I didn't really own anything. My credit card did!

Even when I purchased a designer item on sale, the fact of the matter is, I often paid more than the cost after accounting for the interest that lingered on my credit card. And the sad reality is, although my designer bags were quite trendy, they were lonely because I didn't have any cash to place into them!

If you are at a place where you may have the latest gadget, designer bag, or smartphone, but don't have a matching savings account, it is time to make a change! Before my B.C. (before cash) days, I had to admit that I had a spending problem. While my outward appearance was simply beautiful because I was "dressed to the nines," in the latest fashion at all times and eating at fine restaurants, it finally dawned on me that I couldn't really afford any of it and made a decision to get my finances in order but more importantly, get on a BUDGET!

Write it all out

If you haven't budgeted for a while, it is now time to write it all out! You will never get a handle on your finances if you don't get a handle on your budget. Why?

Because without a budget you are merely playing Russian roulette with your money - month after month. So where do you begin?

Remember, at each payday or once a week (if you are self-employed), take some to write out all of your income and expenses for the period. As you recall in Chapter 1, I suggest making this a habit, where you start first with prayer – asking God for His wisdom before executing your spending plan a.k.a. budget.

The budget basics

So first, what is a budget? A **budget** is simply a roadmap or guide. Remember, not only is it important to budget to keep your cash in check, but a budget can help you reach your financial goals. Think about it. If you don't have a plan for your money, you will only come up short or find yourself in a deficit.

As a result, you will have to continue to borrow against future income. If this cycle continues, you will be unable to reach your financial goals, such as saving for a rainy day, investing or purchasing your dream home.

Therefore, a budget is simply a listing of your expected cash inflows and outflows. Your **cash inflows** are income items you expect to receive for a certain period. These items may include your salaries and wages, rental income, investments, business earnings and other sources of income. **Cash outflows** are expenses paid during a certain period. Mortgage or rent payments, utilities, savings, and groceries are examples of cash outflows.

Cash outflows could be further classified into discretionary or nondiscretionary expenses. **Discretionary** expenses are not essential to your budget and could be eliminated if necessary. For example, items such as entertainment or dining out are considered non-essential and are discretionary expenses.

It is a good idea to reduce or eliminate discretionary expenses to help you reach your financial goals. On the other hand, expenses that are essential to your budget are considered **nondiscretionary**. These expenses may include utilities, mortgage payments, food and other essential items. Unlike discretionary expenses, these expenses cannot be eliminated.

Keep in mind, the process of budgeting involves determining whether you will have a **net cash surplus** or **deficit** at the end of the period. A net cash surplus occurs when the expected cash inflows exceed cash outflows. A net cash deficit occurs when the expected cash outflows are more than cash inflows. If you are operating in a deficit, it is time to take a real look at your expenses to determine which ones can be reduced or eliminated.

Cash flow is key

Whether you are operating in a deficit or surplus, there are still some adjustments you are required to make. Increasing your cash flow is essential to help you to reach your goals. This is key if you want to pay down debt, save for a rainy day or anything else. It is also essential because it allows for a cushion and gives you the opportunity to break financial bondage.

One way to increase your bottom line is to audit your expenses. Go through each expense and determine what expenses can be cut or eliminated. If you are paying $200 to your cable bill but $0 to your savings, this can't be!!! I often say – know that – no one deserves your money better than you!

Keep making changes so that you can find an additional surplus in your budget. I have spoken about this in the introduction but think it's important to also mention it now. During the time I wanted to pay off debt, I understood it would only be possible if I was able to stay within my budget.

Why? Because many times on paper – we are quick to say I only pay $100 for dining but the fact is if we are true to ourselves, we spend well above this amount. However, sticking to our budget allows "that imaginary cash flow" to become a reality.

How to use the B.A.D.G.E.® Budget Worksheet

After you have determined what items should be included, it is time to get to work! Take a few minutes out of your day and create a realistic budget. Using your past financial history and expected cash inflows and outflows, **utilize the B.A.D.G.E.® – Budget worksheet.**

First, list your salary, rental and investment income and other cash flows for the pay period. Next, list your expected cash outflows. This should include expenses you expect to pay for the pay period. Expenses may include tithes, mortgage or rent, utilities, cell phone bills, childcare, auto, insurance and other expenses.

Finally, determine whether you have a surplus or net deficit. If you have determined that you are operating at a deficit or simply desiring additional income, please read my article, *21 Ways to Save*. *https://kemberley.com/21-ways-to-save/*

Reflection

Meet with your partner and discuss the importance of preparing and writing your budget for the period. What areas require special attention?

START WITH ABCS!

Proverbs 9:10

CHAPTER 3

Building Block #3:

Start with ABCs!

The fear of the Lord is the beginning of wisdom...

(Proverbs 9:10 KJV)

Let's just say you received a sum of money or better yet – it is payday! What is the first thing you do? Do you just hit the ground running as it relates to paying your bills, shelling out cash to the kids or spending on the things you desire? Or do you create a plan for your money?

We all know that we should budget, but the fact of the matter is many of us simply neglect to do it. But if we are to be good stewards of the finite resources we have, we simply must count the cost at all times (Haggai 1:7)!

So what do you do if simply hate to budget? Have no fear. If budgeting is really not your "thing," there is still hope!

When I speak to groups, I often ask – "How many in this room prepare a budget?" I am always shocked by the one or two people who actually raise their hands! Now, while I am shocked – I do not judge. Why? Because for a long time I thought winging it would get me to a better financial place. However, there is simply no way around it. If you want to get your finances in order you have to start with a budget.

This holds true not only in our financial lives but also of all areas in our lives as well. I once heard a preacher say, "Many people want the victory but are not willing to do the work!" That was an "aha" moment for me in my life. It made me think, what are some things I am asking God for that I am not taking the necessary steps? Better put – place yourself in position!

If you want to create a great business, it means you have to put in hours of work. If you want to be an expert in your field, it means you have to sacrifice time to study. If you want to build better relationships, you have to take the time to invest in your family and loved ones that are around you today.

There is no way around it. Think of the great people in your life who are doing great things. Chances are, they are not wasting their time but taking the time to make sacrifices to ensure they have a better future!

This is no different with our finances. No matter if you are "balling" or simply living paycheck to paycheck, you have to create a budget for your finances in order to obtain a financial healing. Remember, your finances should be decent and in order at all times (1 Corinthians 14:40).

The ABCs to budgeting

Some people shy away from budgeting because they think it has to be complicated. But remember, your system does not have to be complicated, just simple and easy to use. An easy approach to track your finances is to separate your money into three "money piles," which I like to refer to as A-B-C!

Remember, after you have set aside a time to seek God's wisdom through prayer, paid your tithes and have an idea of your budget, it is time to simplify it.

A – Automate Savings

Pay yourself first! If you have struggled in the past with savings, set up an auto draft where your money is withdrawn directly from your account with little to no effort. Also, if you simply lack discipline, consider using accounts where it would take an "act of Congress" to get your money!

Placing your savings habit on auto pilot can make certain you have something set aside for a rainy day, no matter how big or small. This will allow you to save with no extra thought. Remember, it doesn't have to be large amounts but you must however be consistent. Saving a little can add up big over time.

B – Bill Management

Next, write out a listing of all your bills you are required to pay for the period. For instance, if you are paid twice per month, I recommend creating a budget according to your pay dates. I often refer to this as **paycheck budgeting.** This simply means each time you are paid you budget only for that period.

Keep in mind, if you are self-employed, it may be a good idea to create a weekly budget for your finances to help you stay abreast of not only expenses but your revenue goals.

Next, total your bill amounts and pay this total on the day you are paid. This way the only money remaining in your account would be for discretionary spending or reaching a certain financial goal. This will reduce the amount of late fees or the need to remember when bills are due because of various due dates.

C- Cash for Everything Else

Finally, after you have determined the amount you need to tithe, save and spend on monthly bills, whatever remains is yours for the "keeping." This is a great method because not only have you already paid your bills but you have saved money for the future and now you should be able to enjoy the remainder of your hard earned cash the way you want!

Now, keep in mind, for the purpose of this book, I discuss budgeting principles only. But you should consider setting up your 401(k) and retirement savings as part of your budget.

Making it simple! Money Piles

So now that you are armed with an easier way to budget, let's talk about how simple you can make it. Consider thinking about the ABCs to budgeting as placing your money into three money piles.

Let's say for instance you receive your net pay of $2,000. This is your pay after shelling out payroll taxes, paying your tithes, and any deductions such as your company's 401(k). Now you are ready to get your budget on!
So let's get busy, shall we?

Consider setting aside ten percent (10%) for emergencies. In this case, setting aside $200 is appropriate, which will leave you with $1,800. Next, add up your bills for the period. As you can recall, this is referred to as paycheck budgeting. If you have $1,200 of bills for the period, you then will be left with $600. This is your cash for "everything else."

This could be for shopping, dining out, entertainment and more. It can also be to help a family member who needs assistance, reach a financial goal and anything else!

The great thing about using this method is – it is simple and easy to use. Consider using this the next time you are paid.

How to use the B.A.D.G.E. ® ABCs worksheet

One great way to simplify your budget is to utilize the **B.A.D.G.E. ® – ABCs Worksheet**. This worksheet provides you with an opportunity to create three money piles for your finances.

Recall the three steps using the acronym – ABCs

- Set up automatic payments to save towards your financial goals.

- Get an idea of the amount of bills you have for the period and pay these on the date you are paid.

- Utilize the remaining cash to reach a financial goal or discretionary spending.

Take time to determine the amount of income you are expected to receive for a period. Using the same period, determine the amount you expect to save automatically, which bills are due and the amount of cash that remains after satisfying your obligations.

Reflection

Meet with your partner and discuss the ABCs to budgeting. Discuss how implementing this method can simplify your finances.

START WITH TRACKING!

Haggai 1:5-7

CHAPTER 4

Building Block #4:

Start with tracking!

Now therefore, thus says the Lord of hosts, "Consider your ways! You have sown much, but harvest little; you eat, but there is not enough to be satisfied; you drink, but there is not enough to become drunk; you put on clothing, but no one is warm enough; and he who earns, earns wages to put into a purse with holes." Thus says the Lord of hosts, "Consider your ways!

(Haggai 1:5-7 NASB)

Have you ever opened your Bible and fell on a scripture and knew immediately God was speaking to you? If you are a person who spends time with God, there are times you know He is speaking directly to you! This was the case when I first read this scripture many years ago.

I knew God was saying, "Get it together!" Again –
another "aha" moment!

You make a lot but how much do you keep

This section's scripture is powerful. It tells us to
consider our ways! It reminds us that we make much
but only keep a little! I like to say, "You make a lot
of money, but how much do you keep?"

The first time I read this scripture, I felt as if God
was right before my eyes asking me the very same
question. The conviction was real! But let me ask
you, "Are your pockets deep but have holes in
them?" At the end of the month, do you question
where your money has gone? Are you able to
account for your daily spending and have a sense of
where each dollar has been allocated?

The only way to a financial healing is having an idea of what you are spending on a periodic basis and determine what areas may need adjusting. However, this can only be achieved through the power of tracking your finances.

Tracking your expenses provides a great reality check. Most often, as we create our budgets we might say we only spend a certain amount on a line item. However, when we review our bank statements, credit cards and other payment methods, we quickly realize we spend a whole lot more!

When I meet with clients as it relates to getting their finances in order, I often start with a simple exercise. I instruct them to review the past thirty (30) days and list every single item they paid for during that time. Most often, they are amazed regarding the amount of money they spent. And even more amazed about charges to their accounts that they simply were not aware!

Just think, if they monitored on a regular basis, they would be more likely to save more or reach a financial goal! But this type of financial healing can only be achieved through the power of tracking your finances!

Track now

How do you track your finances? What is the best way to achieve this? This may be difficult if you have been living your life without taking the time out to monitor your morning latte!

Recall, I discussed an easy way to budget in Chapter 3 – the ABCs. This is a great place to start. If you have followed this principle, this is an example of how your B-A-D-G-E ® Money Tracker Sheet would look like. Let's say your after-tax paycheck is $2,000 per period. After you have paid your tithes and sought God's direction, you should record your automated savings, bills and cash for everything else.

Cash doesn't necessarily mean you have to go without the use of a debit card, but this is the amount remaining to take care of discretionary expenses.

Name	Category	Amount	Balance
Balance	Balance	--	$2,000
Savings	Savings	($200)	$1,800
Bills	Bills	($1,200)	$600
Cash	Dining	($20)	$580
Cash	Gasoline	($40)	$540
Cash	Shopping	($60)	$480

Consider your ways!

Tracking is not only for the purposes of accounting for your finances, but is definitely for the purpose of identifying problem spending areas. This is key to obtaining a financial healing. Not only are identifying leaks in your finances crucial, but "putting the brakes" on this type of spending can help your finances as well. Consider this. If you are spending an extra $30 per day, this could amount to $900 per month of extra spending in your budget!

Think about it! This extra spending could be used to reach some of your financial goals. Simply saving this amount monthly can help pad an emergency fund in the amount of ten thousand eight hundred dollars ($10,800) per year! I am certain you can use an extra ten thousand ($10,000) a year!

This is why it is so important to identify what's draining your wallet. Most often, these sneaky expenses that are draining our wallets are usually **discretionary expenses**. As discussed before, discretionary expenses are simply expenses that are not essential to your budget. Examples of these types of expenses include dining out, impulsive purchases, shopping, your morning coffee latte and sometimes your family and friends!

Whatever it is, it is time to get your spending under control. You have to make a serious effort to reduce or eliminate these expenses so that you stay on budget. It really comes down to understanding what you can and cannot afford!

Create spending limits

Now that you have identified spending areas that have drained your wallet, it is now time to place a limit on your spending. Having a budget or financial plan doesn't mean you have to eliminate certain expenses, but it does mean to get control over your spending. For instance, if you love to shop, determine how much "shopping" you can truly afford!

Yes, you may feel as though you deserve that brand new gadget or another pair of pumps, but you have to determine whether you really can afford it. Understanding beforehand is ideal because this way, you are not just buying anything each month, but you are taking your time, praying and getting a handle on your spending. This will actually help you in the long run!

Because you, my friend, are a person who is selective and buying the best items for your buck!

Be true to thyself

Lastly, be true to thyself! Monitor your spending and determine whether you should limit or eliminate certain expenses from your budget. Ask yourself the hard questions about your spending habits. Also, if you know you can't afford something, simply do not buy it! Petition God for discipline and contentment. This can help you to avoid spending on items that you simply may not need.

It is so important to identify what's draining your wallet.

@Kemwashcpa

#kemcents

How to use the B.A.D.G.E. ®
Money Tracker

Tracking your spending will not only help you to stay within your budget, but can also help you to identify the following:

- Whether you are spending within your means;

- Identify spending areas you should reduce or eliminate; and/or

- Reallocate monies used for certain items towards a financial goal.

One great way to track your spending is to record your purchases utilizing the B.A.D.G.E. ® – Money Tracker. This worksheet provides you with an opportunity to record amounts spent daily. Keep it with you throughout the day. Periodically, review your expenses to determine whether you are spending within your budget. Carefully monitor and determine what expenses should be eliminated to help you obtain your financial healing.

Reflection

Meet with your partner and discuss the money tracking principle. Identify one expense you are committed to reduce or eliminate. How will this impact your financial situation?

START WITH YOUR BILLS!

1 Corinthians 14:40

CHAPTER 5

Building Block #5:

Start with your bills in order!

Let all things be done decently and in order.

1 Corinthians 14:40 (NKJV)

From month to month, we are responsible to pay bill after bill. And for many, if a bill payment system is not put in place, you may find yourself off track. Having a bill payment system is extremely important.

This is simply a structure set in place so that you know whom you owe, when bills are due and whether payments have been made. No matter if you are paying your bills manually or using an auto draft option, which allows bills to be automatically deducted from your bank account, having a bill payment system in place can help you obtain financial healing.

First things first, get organized! Remember, all things should be done decently and in proper order (1 Corinthians 14:40). How is your bill payment system? Are you operating "out of order?" If you are not up to par, don't worry. Apply the tips discussed in this chapter and commit to obtaining a financial healing over your bills.

No need for the guessing game

First, get an understanding of all of your **recurring bills** for the period, which are bills expected to be received on a continuous monthly basis. Most often these recurring bills are for **fixed expenses**, which means the amount remains consistent. However, these bills could also be for **variable expenses**, which means the amounts could change from period to period. For example, your cell phone services may be considered a variable expense if the amount is based on usage.

For many of us, our bills are the same each and every month. So there should not be a guessing game as it relates to your bills!

Without a sound system in place, we may never have a true understanding of whom we owe. Gather previous bills and get a realistic idea of all bills that are due each month. Also, get an understanding of bills that may be lingering from your past. If you are responsible for past bills, commit to paying a determined amount monthly to ensure you are able to reduce or eliminate these expenses by your target date.

Put a system in place

At the beginning of each month or pay period, take a moment to review current bills due for the period. Consider using a **paycheck bill system.** This simply means paying your bills on the day you are paid or consider paying weekly if you are self-employed.

For instance, if you are paid twice per month – on the first (1st) and the fifteenth (15th), it is a good idea to separate your bills into two categories. Bills that are due at the beginning of the period (1st through 15th) and bills that are due at the end of the period (16th through 30th).

Therefore, bills that are due between the first (1st) and the fifteenth (15th) should be paid on the first (1st). Whereas bills that are due between the fifteenth (15th) and thirtieth (30th), should be paid on the fifteenth (15th).

Paying your bills in this manner, not only allows you to pay your bills timely but also helps to avoid late fees. In addition, it reduces the chances of forgetting to pay your bills, because remember life happens. Also, consider making notes for unexpected bills that you may receive throughout the period and include them in your current bills.

Lastly, now that you know whom you owe for the period, make a listing of your bills that you are responsible for and mark as paid when payment is made.

21 Ways to Save

If you have ever taken my class, you will know I always stress for participants to review their bills and find ways to save more money. I have a list on my website that discusses tips in detail, but we will go into some tips now.

Insurance costs

Review insurance policies and shop around for the best price. Now keep in mind, you should consider the insurance company's rating before switching. In addition, while a higher deductible could reduce your premium, if you are not careful, the amount may be too high and can cause a financial stress if you don't have the funds to pay the deductible. Speak to your insurance professional first before making any decisions. Also, don't forget to ask about multiline discounts for multiple policies.

Cable and Internet Services

Take time to review your cable and internet services and determine ways to reduce your expenses. If you are paying a high cable or internet bill, you have to do something about it. Especially if you are paying the provider more than what you have set aside for monthly savings. I often say, "No one deserves your money better than you!" Determine what services you need and consider making a change. Remember, it is a good idea to contact your service provider and ask whether there are discounts or customer loyalty programs that can reduce your costs.

Credit card interest

It may be a good idea to reach out to credit card companies to determine whether interest rates can be reduced. This could definitely work in your favor if you have been a long time customer and your credit has improved since you first opened the line of credit. Remember, it does not hurt to ask! Even the Bible reminds us that we should ask if we expect to receive (Matthew 7:7).

Delete one bill and save

Lastly, review all of your bills and delete one expense. If you are signed up for services you may no longer need or simply not using, consider slashing it. The extra cash could be used for saving or reaching a financial goal. So get at it and pay less and save more!

How to use the B.A.D.G.E. ® Bill Calendar Worksheet

Each payday or weekly, identify which bills are owed for the period. If you have been playing the "guessing game" when it comes to your finances, it is time to make a change. Utilize the B.A.D.G.E. ® Bill Calendar, which serves as a reminder for your bills. The B.A.D.G.E. ® Bill Calendar allows you to:

- List each bill for the period;

- Record the amount due and due date for each bill;

- Categorize bills by type;

- Mark bills when paid manually or auto draft; and

- Provides a snapshot of all bills owed for a certain period.

Most importantly, keep your bill calendar visible. Place it somewhere you can see it daily to help keep your finances on track.

Reflection

Discuss your bill paying system with your partner. No matter if you have a few bills or a lot, without a sound system in place they can be overwhelming. The key to getting a handle on your bills is to ensure you create and utilize a bill payment calendar at the onset of each pay period. What areas do you need to adjust concerning your bills?

START WITH KNOWING!

Proverbs 1:5

CHAPTER 6

Building Block #6:

Start with knowing

A wise man will hear, and will increase learning; and a man of understanding shall attain unto wise counsels:

(Proverbs 1:5 KJV)

One of the most challenging things I ever had to deal with in my life was Hurricane Katrina. But not only the impact of the storm but the stroke my father suffered shortly afterwards. I remembered spending time with my dad just a day or two before. We went to one of my favorite places to eat and just talked and laughed about really much of nothing, but we had such a great time.

But things really did change from that moment. My dad was hospitalized shortly afterwards for more than thirty days. It was those days in the hospital, my family and I prayed like no other. The doctors said he would never be able to walk again and have slurred speech for the rest of his life. But through

God's grace – He is not only walking but has so much to say (seriously)!

During that time, my family and I heard what the doctor's report stated. However, we placed our trust in the ultimate Doctor above! So we prayed. I mean really prayed. I can recall my mother instructing my siblings and I to read the Book of Romans, Chapter 10, seven (7) times for seven (7) days. After a month or so, my dad was released and that moment alone made me realize the great power of our God!

Move from the unknown zone

But here is the thing. It was also in that moment, I realized that we were all in the "unknown zone." This may be the zone you too may be operating with your family as well. See up until that moment, I had no idea about some of my dad's personal finances. So right there – as my dad was recovering from a stroke, I had to ask him the tough questions such as:

Dad, who holds your mortgage?

Who is your insurance carrier?

What bills are you responsible for this month?

...and the list can go on and on!

It was in this moment that I realized something. It is extremely important to let someone know about your finances.

So have you? If you had a disaster, will all of your financial information be in one place? Would you be able to tell someone to simply go home, grab my folder and bring it to the hospital? Or would your loved ones be at a lost with nowhere to turn?

Have the discussion

Now listen, I am not saying everybody has to know everything! But you do need to select one or two persons, that in the event of an emergency, who will know your desires and some financial information concerning your financial affairs to ensure things go smoothly. Remember, you are not just doing this just for you, but you are doing this for them as well! It is a good idea to pick someone who may live in your home, but also someone who lives outside of

your home. This is a good practice just in case
something happens simultaneously to you and
those who may reside with you.

Next, it is a good idea to place all of your important
financial paperwork into one place. This is helpful
in the event you have an emergency and need to
grab your documents quickly and go.

Yearly Check-up

Last but not least, you should review your items
periodically, possibly annually. This way you can
determine whether updates are needed. Times
change, needs change and more importantly,
relationships change as well. Taking the time to
check current beneficiaries and what policies are
still in place is essential. In addition, determine what
your policy covers. This way, when the time comes
you are not caught off guard due to inadequate
coverage!

Preparing for the unexpected

Hurricane Katrina also taught me another lesson. I had only been out of college just a few years and never would have guessed I would have to go through such a huge disaster. I can recall right before traveling out of town to evacuate (young and naïve), I grabbed a few things and made certain that my CPA license was safe and sound, but really had no clue exactly how my life was about to change. That lesson taught me so much!

Save something (always!)

For starters, it taught me the importance of saving. You have to save something no matter what! This is why budgeting is so important. If you don't stick to your budget – chances are – you may not have the extra money to save for a rainy day. If you have not set up a savings account, it is imperative to do so immediately. If you are in a place where you may feel that you do not have the means to save, continue to explore options, such as finding ways to increase income, slashing expenses from your budget, seeking professional help and more importantly asking God for His help and guidance. He promises in His Word to be our helper (Psalm 121:1)!

Keep in mind, saving is a lot different from investing. Your savings account should be liquid and easy to get to in case of an emergency. As such, you should seek out high yield savings accounts to stash your cash. Also, it is a good idea to get an understanding of just how much money you should set aside for savings.

A great way to determine your emergency savings goal is to determine the amount of nondiscretionary expenses you have on a monthly basis. Recall from Chapter 2, that your nondiscretionary expenses include items such as your mortgages, car loans, utilities, insurances and other necessities. After you have determined the monthly amount, calculate the amount needed for at least three to six months. This number will result in the amount required for your emergency savings.

Create a checklist

Lastly, as you prepare for the unexpected, begin to gather certain financial items that may be required in the event of a disaster. Here is a checklist that I created shortly after Hurricane Katrina. But don't just stop here. Adjust this list as needed and update it frequently.

Financial Disaster Checklist

Financial Disaster Checklist

	Yes	No	N/A
1. Cash (ATMs may not be available)	☐	☐	☐
2. Birth Certificates	☐	☐	☐
3. Passports	☐	☐	☐
4. Social Security Cards	☐	☐	☐
5. Credit Cards	☐	☐	☐
6. Savings Bonds	☐	☐	☐
7. Military Identification	☐	☐	☐
8. Shot Records	☐	☐	☐
9. Degrees	☐	☐	☐
10. Certificates/Licenses	☐	☐	☐
11. Resumes	☐	☐	☐
12. Financial Statements	☐	☐	☐
13. Wills	☐	☐	☐
14. Title/Deeds	☐	☐	☐
15. Tax Returns	☐	☐	☐
16. Insurance Policies	☐	☐	☐
17. Prescriptions	☐	☐	☐
18. Power of Attorney	☐	☐	☐
19. Vehicle Registration	☐	☐	☐
20. Important Pictures/Valuables	☐	☐	☐

Kimberley.com
Remember, Your Choice, Your Future!

How to use the B.A.D.G.E. ®
Financial Disaster Checklist

Using the B.A.D.G.E. ® Financial Disaster
Checklist, gather the items listed. Place the items in
an accordion folder, binder or portable file
container.

As you prepare for the unexpected, make certain
to take the following steps:

- Review insurance policies with an agent;

- Update and review beneficiaries on financial
  and insurance accounts;

- Determine if you have enough for an
  emergency;

- Take pictures of personal belongings and
  save in the event of a disaster; and

- Update wills and other pertinent
  documents.

Remember, review your financial disaster checklist
annually with a trusted loved one.

Reflection

Take time to determine whether or not you have a financial emergency plan. Consider gathering financial documents that may be necessary in case of a disaster. Have a discussion with a trusted loved one regarding your wishes in the event of an emergency. Discuss with your partner any "to do's" you need to consider, such as creating a will, obtaining insurance, and other steps.

START WITH YOUR GOAL!

Psalm 20:4

CHAPTER 7

Building Block #7:

Start with your goal in mind

May he give you the desire of your heart and make all your plans succeed.

(Psalm 20:4 NIV)

My mom raised my siblings and I on a fixed budget as a single mother. Her one goal was that her children become successful. It was her prayer to God for as long as I can remember. Because of this, she sacrificed everything for us. I mean everything! I can recall my mother working various jobs (all at once) with her end goal in mind. More importantly, she sacrificed her wants to make certain we had everything we need (and sometimes we had a few things we wanted as well!)

Sacrifice today for tomorrow's success

During our time of growing up, my mother would see to it that we recite Psalm 23 daily on our way to school – three times consecutively. I witnessed her waking up early each morning to ensure she spent time with God before starting her day. While these sacrifices meant little to me at the time, as I grew older and began to take on the responsibilities of adulthood, I wondered sometimes – how did she do it all?

See, my mother knew a thing or two about sacrifice. She sacrificed her sleep to spend more time with God. She sacrificed her finances to ensure we were well kept. I can say today, her sacrifices paid off well. My siblings and I did graduate from college and became successful professionals. It was her daily walk with Christ that led us to where we are today.

And this is the kind of sacrifice we too must have if we are going to see a change in our financial situation. We must not do the same things that have drained our finances in the past but move to the place where God is calling us to be as it relates to our finances. This may mean sacrificing spending here or there to ensure we meet a financial goal. It may mean sacrificing funds to ensure we are able to tithe. It may also mean sacrificing time from the things we love to sit down and review our budgets to ensure we are planning for our financial future.

But where can we start?

Create a P.O.W.E.R. goal

We must start with our end goal in mind. When I wanted to get out of credit card debt, I remember making a clear determination that I would reach my goal by a certain date. More importantly, I understood exactly how much money it would take for me to reach my goal.

When I encourage others about reaching their financial goals, I often share this concept that I created many years ago. I often referred to it as a P.O.W.E.R. goal! It simply means:

- Pray and plan over your goal

- One specific goal
- Write it out
- Empower it with action
- Read it daily

For me, creating a P.O. W.E.R. goal has helped me to stay within budget, because I knew if I was able to spend within my limits, I would have the funds needed to pay down my debt.

So what's your goal?

Do you want to save for your children's education? Do you want to simply have a rainy day fund? Do you want to get an idea of what it will take in order to transform your finances? Well first, you must start with a prayer and a plan.

Pray and plan

There is a scripture in the Bible that tells us without a vision the people shall perish (Proverbs 29:18)! This is no different for our lives. If we don't have a clear distinction where we are headed we will never be able to reach our goals. Take time to pray about the goals you desire to accomplish.

Next, ponder on what it would take for you to reach your goal. For instance, when I wanted to pay out my credit card debt within a year, I made a plan to earn additional income to meet my target goal. So let's say for instance if you want to payout a debt of $12,000 per year, make a plan to earn additional income of $1,000 per month. This can be accomplished through obtaining a part-time job, selling assets, or turning your passion into a paycheck. Remember, you have to put in the work. The Bible reminds us that faith without works is dead (James 2:14-26)!

One specific goal

Now if you are anything like me, you want to do a million things at once! But the reality is - concentrating on one thing at a time is more effective than being all over the place. So take a step back and breathe. Remember, Rome wasn't built overnight! While you may want to accomplish a few financial goals at once, try your best to concentrate on one goal at a time.

Write it down

I absolutely love writing! And writing out your goals is a great way to help them to come to pass. I believe there is power when we put our thoughts to paper. So much so, I write prayers to God each morning. I am often amazed when I review my past prayers! More importantly, I am grateful for all of the prayers He has answered and the direction He continues to provide for me!

Empower it with action

Once you have an idea of what that goal may be – attack your goal with your plan of action. Each day take a step towards your goal. Make the sacrifices it will take to help you bring it to pass. Remember, it is important to not only pray about your goal but put the right actions in place so that you can see your goals to the finish line.

Read it daily

Remember, not only write out your goal, but put it somewhere you are able to see it daily. For instance, place it on your mirror that you utilize when dressing daily. If you are a spender, place your financial goal on your debit or credit card before swiping! This may reduce the amount of money you spend. Whatever the case, simply place it somewhere you are able to see it every day.

Finally, the only way to make this work is that you put in WORK! There is no success without sacrifice! Remember, faith without works is dead! So do what is needed and you will see a true change in your finances!

How to use the B.A.D.G.E. ®
Goals Worksheet

First, list out your goals using the B.A.D.G.E. ®
Goals Worksheet. Next, determine the date you
expect the goal to come to pass. Lastly, write out
your action plan to make your goals come to pass.

This sheet allows you to:

- Keep your goals visible;

- Stay accountable regarding your target
  dates;

- Create a plan of action to help your goals
  become a reality;

- Track your progress monthly; and

- Provides a snapshot of all your goals in one
  place.

Remember, write out your vision and make it plain
(Habakkuk 2:2). It shall definitely run if you put in
the necessary work!

Reflection

Discuss your goal with your partner. List a few things that have kept you from reaching your goal. Next, determine how you will overcome each. Incorporate the P.O.W.E.R. steps to help you reach your goal.

About the Author

Kemberley "Kemcents" Washington is a certified public accountant, financial news contributor and a best seller author. She started her career with the Internal Revenue Service (IRS) as both a revenue agent and criminal investigator. Subsequently, she decided to embark on her own, where she provides financial services and education to others through her business.

She has written *21 Days of Powerful Breakthroughs* and *The Ten Commandments to a Financial Healing* and more. Her books are featured on the *YouVersion Bible App* and have more than 200,000 downloads collectively. Most often, you can find Kemberley on the news, writing a piece for a major media outlet or simply sharing a tip on her blog, Kemberley.com.